Andrew Staniland was born in Sheffield in 1959 and lives in London, where he works part time. His books so far have been self-published (poetry collections, narrative poems, prose-poem novels and plays).

titles by the author:

Playful Poems
Rhapsodies (2014)
The Perennial Poetry (2010)
Two Story Poems (2009)
Hymns, Films And Sonnetinas (2007)
New Poems (2006)
The Beauty Of Psyche (2005)
The Weight Of Light (2004)
Three Cine-Poems (1997)
Poems (1982-2004)
Four Plays (1994)

Andrew Staniland

Playful Poems

published 2018 by
Andrew Staniland's Books

www.andrewstaniland.co.uk

© Andrew Staniland 2016

cover design by the author
photo of the author by Robert Garbolinski

ISBN 978-0-244-97226-4

Contents

The Taming Of The Shrew
1.	I word it better than I woo	1
2.	Although no dowry now, no deed	1
3.	Re: wonderment and watts	1

Richard III
4.	A conniving crookback of a king	2
5.	The way to sell a lie	2
6.	An old and alcoholic king	3
7.	It won't be *cast the die*	3
8.	The choruses of muddy crones	4

The Comedy Of Errors
9.	The arbiter of *if* is *when*	4
10.	These twins I am, the two of me	5

Love's Labour's Lost
11.	I am in love, but not	6
12.	Those numbers that are prime	7

Richard II
13.	The hand of state	8
14.	The price of pride	9
15.	The attribute of conscience in a king	9
16.	A minister of shadows, voted out	9

Romeo And Juliet

17.	The boys in black	10
18.	Well, I was rubbish as a Romeo	11
19.	The *rasa* on my lips from reading this	11
20.	The old should die before the young	12

A Midsummer Night's Dream

21.	Wild times! I know a ditch in Walthamstow	12
22.	Intriguing me, a hum I hear	13
23.	The lovely wood of piebald light	14
24.	The pink and yellow palette of the dawn	15
25.	A centaur has a human head	15

The Merchant Of Venice

26.	The instinct to survive	16
27.	A reckless wreck	17
28.	*No debt!*	17
29.	It is a fine thing to forgive	18

Henry IV Part One

30.	A politician who is pure	18
31.	A hero's weapon was a sword, a spear	19
32.	A father who finds fame	19
33.	A horse on stage is not a horse	20

Henry IV Part Two

34.	And they negotiated through the night	20
35.	A smirk of smoke	21
36.	An honest heir is drilled to do	21

The Merry Wives Of Windsor

37.	An Englishwoman of a certain vintage	22
38.	And walking on a wetland by the sea	23

Much Ado About Nothing

39.	I want a wife, a wife in white	24
40.	The silence of a smile	25

Henry V

41.	An inner source of light	25
42.	A street-fighter of the right	26
43.	The grandsons of the medal-chested men	27
44.	The fashions and the fun	27
45.	I was a boy	28

Julius Caesar

46.	A country needs a casting vote	29
47.	Well played! An inn-	29
48.	The cosmos that a country is	30
49.	A private hate because of x	30
50.	A poet knows the proper names	30

As You Like It

51.	The refugees had hidden in the forest	31
52.	The well-judged stage	31
53.	A lark of love	32

Hamlet

54.	Let's say I see a ghost	33
55.	Like shadows from the n-stones at Stonehenge	33
56.	Why spy	34
57.	Arjuna asked, to fight or not to fight	35
58.	A daughter has to disobey	36
59.	*The quotes!*	36
60.	I call a corpse a corpse. It seemed to me	37

Twelfth Night

61.	Out of the early blue, on an Aegean shore	37
62.	The love of listening	38
63.	I trust that neither distance's disguise	38

Troilus And Cressida

64.	The reason why they went to war	39
65.	Some of the sentries of the siege	39
66.	The women warriors in green	40

Othello

67.	Those rivals of the Renaissance	41
68.	A fifty-something fool	42
69.	Imagination, that illuminates	42
70.	With human evil, I have not	43
71.	With human weakness, I will not	44

Measure For Measure

72.	With sex, we have to conjugate	45
73.	A gutter press is looking up	45
74.	*The pear is slumping from its lot*	46

All's Well That Ends Well

75.	A heroine	47
76.	His first war, he was scared	48

King Lear

77.	No rights, no rules	48
78.	*Who am I?* What a question for a king	49
79.	To feel	50
80.	And when a storm of light	50
81.	The casting for Cordelia is *small*	51

Macbeth

82.	These weird ones are a rival rule	52
83.	The tyrant's wife is taut and tanned	52
84.	The most efficient means	53
85.	A politics of hatred, *red is right*	53
86.	The sun is red	54

Antony And Cleopatra

87.	To meditate	55
88.	The stains of lubricants on flannel bedding	55
89.	O what a man he was, a man	56
90.	Bodily beauty isn't why, my friend	57

Coriolanus

91.	A Twitter mob	58
92.	He is polite, professional and *pfff*	59
93.	The power of language, for a populist	59
94.	They called him K, Commander K	60

Cymbeline

95.	The photo is *A Sleeping Nude*	61
96.	And after all those tragedies	62

The Winter's Tale

97.	A risk that isn't real	63
98.	She picks a stem in pink, in pink	63
99.	Nobody chooses to be changed	64

The Tempest

100.	This island isn't England, it is hot	65
101.	This monster is of man, but isn't man	66
102.	O Ariel	67
103.	A work of art, then, if it works	68

Notes   70

Playful Poems

1.

I word it better than I woo,
    Though what I do today is date,
        Luring a Laura with an O
    Or messing with a miss called Kate.

The nub of this is nothing new,
    A *sesame* from no to yes,
        As Petrarch or Petruchio,
    A pickup artist. *Please undress.*

2.

Although no dowry now, no deed,
    The contract is as crude,
        Who pays/gets paid,
        Who lies/get laid,
And shaking on the contact that I need,
    As I should do if I were shrewd,
    If only I were shrewd.

3.

Re: wonderment and watts,
    And goodness and a god,
What matches me is not
    And even may be odd.

4.

A conniving crookback of a king
   Is knifing backs, a king of crooks,
     With oil as spoils
     And spoils as oil,
Sponging the bloodstains off the bling,
   A black tongue so a critic croaks.

5.

   The way to sell a lie
     Is wink at it and smile,
   Insist and then imply
     It is a view and versatile,

And that is what is on *The Nothing Show*,
The show that shows to know is not to know,

   A screen of stimuli,
     Of psychotropic style
   (The substance to supply
     A *philophobe* or *phobiphile*),

A fool who licks his lips as if to say,
This isn't propaganda, this is play!

6.

An old and alcoholic king
Said, *Do a thing*,
   To cow the crowd.

A thing! Not bombs...
With cold aplomb,
   The king and all the court were cowed.

7.

It won't be *cast the die*,
   A turn, a turn, a turn,
     A tyrant's tyrant, time,
Will tell a tyrant, *Die!*

All eyes on him, all dry,
   An answer from an urn
     Will ask about a crime,
A tyrant has to die.

Red running down like dye,
   A row of burning tyres
     Billowing, acrid black,
Will tell a tyrant, *Die!*

When what is due is due,
   A tyrant can't retire
     And *question at the back*,
A tyrant has to die.

8.

The choruses of muddy crones,
    For all the losses that they mourn,
As if a careless *roué* croons,
      Are nurses of a newer curse
  And from a metal-toothed moraine
      Throw comets onto Mars's course.

9.

The arbiter of *if* is *when*,
    As in the art of farce,
      The timing of the entrances,
The trousers off the arse.

And an untimely *mise en scène*
    Of me, whoops, unentrances…
      Try, try again, a sibyl says,
When isn't what she answers.

10.

These twins I am, the two of me,
    Who seem the same
    And are in name
And are too in anatomy,
        Are not, are truly not.

Twin One is the immortal twin
    (Pollux!) in poems
    Of *lux*, of *Oms*,
Lyricising, without, within,
        And loving it, the lot.

Twin Two, the merely mortal one
    (Bollocks!) in prose,
    Um, comes and goes,
Wearily wasting, on and on,
        For what, if not for what?

And no one knows if who they meet
    Is me, Twin Poet,
    Or me, inchoate,
Which clues mean which, which might be moot,
        Which either has or hasn't got.

11.

I am in love, but not
    With any woman I know,
Albeit I know many who are Helen-hot,
    Who aren't just so-so, no,
    But O-so and just-so.

I am in love, but not
    Even with luminous love,
As luscious as its light is. It is apricot,
    Its sunspots apricots, all of
    What sunlight is through leaves.

I am in love with what
    To write, the loveliest line,
The English ribbon of it, ending in a knot
    Of lines that intertwine,
    Like knotty eglantine.

12.

Those numbers that are prime
    Are elemental things,
As moments are in time,
    The throb of wonder's wings.

The same is true of rhyme,
    An elemental pair
Is also pure and prime,
    An aerial of air.

An ark of names, the heart
    Lets out a homing dove,
Flying, a natural art,
    To find a leaf of love.

And when a rhymed line ends,
    What doesn't is so clear,
So consonant, it sends
    Ananda to the ear.

13.

The hand of state
That hesitates,
   Through decency or doubt,

To sign off on
An op to con-
   Tract toppling a tyrant out,

   Will mop what spills
   And what it spoils
      In an emergency.

*

From truncheons' thuds
To screeching Scuds,
   A shudder to a shout,

As barrel bombs
(An Arab Somme?)
   Sneeze chlorine from their snouts,

   A flotsam fleet,
   Too full to float,
      Is floundering at sea.

14.

The price of pride,
As prophesied,
   Is peace and pluralism.

An honest umpire
Of an ex-empire,
   A polarising prism.

15.

The attribute of conscience in a king
   Isn't an absolute, an either/or,
It is a re-adjusting, reasoning
   Amidst the rage and ruin of a war.

16.

A minister of shadows, voted out,
   Sidled into the light to say *adieu*,
To all the calculating, all the clout,
   And what he said was honest and was true.

The iron plates of power in the mind,
   The message on, the *n*th point of the plan...
He smiled. He wasn't (though he had) resigned
   And seemed a smaller but more rounded man.

17.

The boys in black
Attack, attack
   The great sacked city Ur.

   The girls of Ur
   Are gifts of myrrh,
A booty for the boys.

Beauty obeys
The boots, the buys,
   With all the caliph cant

   Of boys who can't
   Control a *cunt*,
As Ishtar once was shamed.

The book is blamed,
   The big unborn,
   In God's name, what is sworn.

The boys in black
Go back, go back
   To gameboys and to porn.

18.

Well, I was rubbish as a Romeo,
    The shinning-through-a-window bit,
    The sheet-shy but,
    Come in, I won't bite...
I waited till a woman told me, *No.*

I was too reticent to be requited,
    Too recondite, perhaps, and yet
    I truly met
    A Juliet,
Then boom-boom-boom (as previously cited).

19.

The *rasa* on my lips from reading this
Is a quatrain of hers, of his,
Of soul, sublime, of body, bliss...
It is the *raja yoga* of a kiss.

20.

The old should die before the young
    And peacefully (if poss.),
The other way is war and wrong,
    It is a double loss.

The old are those who order a war,
    The young are those who die,
A toothless house, its splintered door,
    Shell-shattered for no *why*.

21.

Wild times! I know a ditch in Walthamstow,
Where tadpoles swim like sperm and swamp weeds stew,

Beside the sluggish Lea, where barges snooze
And warblers (*little brown jobs*) tweet the news,

Where I am now, a squat, somewhat askew
Few hectares and (*oof!*) a hemisphere of sky.

22.

Intriguing me, a hum I hear
  Of hearing in my inner ear,
Like a gnats' choir, is interrupted by
    A *clang-clunk* of a truck...
    Ah, Puck!

Crafting the iambs of a line,
  As supple as a sapling's spine,
I sense that something is coming... *Ring! Ring! Please buy!*
    No, thanks, goodbye. *Good luck!*
    Ah, Puck!

Although my thighs are soaked and sore,
  The rain's Atlantic rush and roar,
Through the street's seashell, silences me and I
    Am thrilled, am thunderstruck...
    Ah, Puck!

23.

The lovely wood of piebald light
    That any English poem is,
        The spell of it, in root and stem,
Is full of notes from some far summer flight,

    Of figures high on elegance,
        Imagining the outlined leaves
            As metamorphoses from Greece,
    The rays as ruined columns, at a glance,

Of nouns of nature from the north,
    In blackened notches, an unease
        From boggy hollows' wreaths of steam,
Of wizened, wormy windfalls to unearth,

    And *gopis* will run through the wood
        With Krishna on midsummer eves
            And meet Yoruban ghost police
    In odes that are as green as they are good.

24.

The pink and yellow palette of the dawn
    Tickles a lash, a lid,
        To look at *this*, close up, as if
It is a countryside of cheek on down,
    At lips, apart, elide
        An airy light that is the soul of life.

25.

A centaur has a human head
    And horsepower in the rear,
The sort who rapes and is well-read,
    In all ways cavalier.

I am an ass, except the arse,
    And only fit to fart,
Ah, but (big *but*), cue oohs and ahs,
    The bottom of my heart.

26.

The instinct to survive
    Is also for the tribe
And how the tribe survives
    Is over other tribes,

As packs of wolves attack
Wolves of another pack
    That wolfishly intrude
    On one pack's field of food.

*

The impulse to evolve
    Is, fear evolves to love
And love itself evolves
    To empathy that loves

The old foes' fields and flags,
The refugees in rags,
    The ore-veined asteroid,
    The vast ecstatic void.

27.

A reckless wreck,
All on one deck.

Didn't they think?
A ship can sink.

28.

No debt!
No doubt,
But how (as gross
Or net, a gap, a cap, who knows...)
I ask three bald economists
And none agrees, not once, with what each one insists.

No cuts!
The nuts
And bolts of it,
The cost or not, per greasy bit,
I ask three bold economists
And two are pessimistic, one, though, sorry, no, is pissed...

29.

It is a fine thing to forgive,
A fine thing to forgive,

> But if it only follows blame,
> It only follows blame,

And what we get from letting live,
We get from letting live,

> Is something swallowed not sublime,
> Is swallowed not sublime.

30.

A politician who is pure
    Has promised to rule straightly,
A promise that is premature,
    As stiffness isn't stately...
        The crookedness of life, the compromises
        Aren't what will cause a *coup by crisis*.

31.

A hero's weapon was a sword, a spear,
    Then was a musket and a horn,
A shouldered missile and a sack of spares.
        Is this what makes a hero now?

A hero's courage was his strength, his size,
    A berserk brain on top of brawn,
Then cunning and the sharpness of his eyes.
        Is this what makes a hero now?

And in a trench, a summer field's new grid,
    A whistle of incoming warns
A volunteer who crouches, *Grads, lads, Grads!*
        Is this what makes a hero now?

32.

A father who finds fame
And fills a frame,
A fine old flame,
    Shines on, shines on
    And shades a son.

A father, though, who fails,
A fat old fool,
Fiercely fuels
    A son to shun,
    A son to shine.

33.

A horse on stage is not a horse,
    A sword is not a sword.
A horse. A fable of the land, a force.
    A sword. The sound of steel is scored,
    A solo is absurd.

A flag on stage, though, is a flag,
    A crown, though, is a crown.
A flag. A prop for pageants, a red rag.
    A crown. A frill above a frown,
    Like curls on a clown, a clown.

34.

And they negotiated through the night,
    Until at dawn a deal was done,
The *in* of which was neutral, one point nought,
    The *out* of which was, *We have won!*
        The arms of these new lists of knightly skill
        Are audit, argument and utter will.

35.

A smirk of smoke,
A crowy croak,
    And life soon leaks away.

The chubby chops
Of chips, chips, chips,
    And life soon leaks away.

A belly of beer,
A bleary bore,
    And life soon leaks away.

Tick off in time
A class, a climb,
    And life still leaks away.

36.

An honest heir is drilled to do
A job, a job he wants to do.

To do this job, his dad must die,
Must die, as dads must do, some day.

Dead dad! Dead dad! His son is sad.
So soon! So sudden! So he said...

A young king will rule well. Amen.
An old heir is a guilty man.

37.

An Englishwoman of a certain vintage
    (Not *that* old, don't be rude),
Though happy that her haunches have got heavy
    (Not *happy*, dauntless in defeat),
Is still unsure her toenails' lime-green lacquer
    Is *her*, is really *her*.

Is it innate? An English disadvantage?
    Unlike the avian
Italians, the frighteningly French,
    Those snow-tanned Scandinavians,
The gaudy Spanish or the Gouda-y Dutch...

    This winsome Windsor wench
Is also a sophisticate, as such
    (Wines, gins and sundry liquors),
Food would pollute her palate, so no food
    (Those Euro-skinnies *eat*?),
Well, a few nibbles... Bar-ward with her bevy,
    Ah, to be English is to err!

38.

And walking on a wetland by the sea,
    A mile or so from Selsey Bill,
        The wrong side of a reedy stream,
    I think I have to cross it and I will.

    I focus on my fitness, flex my knees
        And leap as if... I splash and slip,
            Not halfway, through a head of slime
        And up a mudslide, sodden to the hip.

No one is near to help me or to see
    The slapstick and the soggy stain,
        So I wring out my self-esteem
    And walk on... *Well, at least I missed the rain.*

    A long leap is performance expertise,
        After is honesty and wit,
            What we remember with a rhyme,
        The way we order and imagine it.

39.

HE (1): I want a wife, a wife in white,
           For one long wedding day,
           Whose *do* will never die
    And who will always wait.

SHE (1): I want a hunky husband for
           The fun, for one long holiday,
           A rutting stag and doe,
    As raw as an affair.

HE (2): I want a witty wife
           For weekdays after work
           And weekends on a walk,
    Who has a warp, who has a woof.

SHE (2): I want a happy hus-
           Band who is always home
           Or heading home, for whom
    The whole of life is only *us*.

40.

The silence of a smile
    Is pointless as a plea
Against an argument of guilt, of guile,
    Only, it seems, a ploy,
    When what is right is a reply.

The silence of a smile,
    As sweetly as it seems
To simper, may be *that, you know, that smell*,
    As if, behind the beam,
    Is something sulphurous, a seam.

*

Even so, though, a sense
    Of silence is a small
Still centre, that is certain of its innocence,
    Infinitesimal-
    Ly sending signals out, as silence smiles.

41.

    An inner source of light
        Surfaces, from the soul,
As sound, a singing of imagination,
    Marking a route, a site,
        And mapping out its role,
Encompassing an image of a nation.

42.

A street-fighter of the right,
    After the April rout,

Runs to the front to fight,
    Flag, rifle, *Fuck off! Out!*

*

Sunflowers fill a field,
    Suddenly it is shelled

And soldierly he shields
    A fellow who is felled.

*

The fanfare that is fit
    For all who fall, who fight,

For him, home after it,
    Out-heroes rules and rights.

43.

The grandsons of the medal-chested men
    Who fought against the fascists in the snow
Are fighting now, with missile, mortar, mine,
    And some of them are friend and some are foe.

The myth of that war is the means of this,
    O monstrous, monstrous! on the evening news,
Although the truth, as ever, isn't thus
    And is a mess of blunders, bribes and booze.

44.

The fashions and the fun
That he fought for are not for him
    And while some smile
    And reconcile,
His fingers feel a gun,
As if it were a phantom limb.

The numbness and the shock,
The sudden speed that spared his life
    For this, re-hired,
    But tired, so tired...
A ticking kitchen clock
Sets it all off. He whacks his wife.

45.

I was a boy
    Who played at war
Behind a palisade of trees,
    A camouflage of corduroy,
Elbows and knees
    Green, grazed and sore.

A clanking king
    Like Harry Five
Was in the field, if not the fray,
    One of the names of reckoning,
Who may or may
    Not be alive.

A boy today
    Is only thumbs,
With ultra-enemies onscreen,
    So many die, so many die,
Quickly and clean-
    Ly, *dum-dum-dum*.

A president,
    At home, destroys,
With a ten million dollar drone,
    A smaller home, by accident,
To dust, a drain
    And two dead boys.

46.

A country needs a casting vote,
    A head that nods, *Yes/No*.
        The head must be on top,
Must have a hat, the hat a coat.

The head must have the confidence
    To nod, if not to know.
        Who wants to (and will stop),
If not who dares to (and who deigns)?

47.

    Well played! An inn-
        Ings ends, is out,
Without a carry-on.

    Those voted in
        Are voted out,
The country carries on.

            *

    A despot does
        What despots do
To a country's carrying-on.

    The despot dies,
        As despots do,
The country carries on.

48.

The cosmos that a country is,
　The pulse of it, its press, its polls,
A despot sets in stone,
As pillars of his throne,
　　And after, in the dust and splintered piles,
　　　The country is in chaos. It is his.

49.

A private hate because of *x*
　Is base, yes, but it has a base,
An axis, *y*, a grind-me axe
　And, as abuse, a time and place.

A public hate that howls *en masse*
　To order is *ex nihilo*
And to it, an anonymous
　Hatee, to whom, alone, *Hello!*

50.

A poet knows the proper names
　Of things, if not his own,
　　Though risk averse,
　　Risking a verse...
O poet, fear the frenzy, fear the fame,
　Fare safely through the streets alone!

51.

The refugees had hidden in the forest,
Where they were out of earshot of the firing squads,
  The roundups of the fittest and the fairest,
The rubble from the Scuds.

  They foraged for its foxes and its weasels,
These supermarket shoppers had to snare and skin,
  Binding young branches, shelters sketched on easels,
Before the frost's first skeins.

  And they were forested, these refugees,
Their coats as dank and mossy as the sunless trunks,
  Their briary beards, their hair's nests twigged with grease,
Skin soil-ingrained, eyes sunk.

52.

  The well-judged stage
    Is what my age
  Should be, *of formal cut*...
      I should be made.

  It isn't. I
    Am not. And why
  I really don't know, but
      I make and am unmade.

53.

A lark of love
    And, no, this isn't
Ornithological, though if...
      No furtive pheasant,
    No duh-duh-dove
Sings so, soars so, on such a riff,

A lark of love
    Is what the wit
Is warmed to when the heart pumps out
      A heady hit,
    To which we groove,
Grinning and being grinned about.

A love of larks
    And, no, I don't
Mean meanness, on the contrary,
      A witty wont,
    Without the snark,
Completely complimentary,

A love of larks,
    Of larks of love,
Takes two, a meeting of true minds,
      To tap its trove,
    Two spirits' sparks
To span its space, two tongues entwined.

54.

Let's say I see a ghost
   Who tells me I must kill
My uncle for a host
   Of reasons, plus the thrill,
And I think, no, I'll wait
   For facts, from someone real,
For an appropriate
   Forum to show some steel,
Why does it mean I'm weak,
   A wobble-board, a wimp?
The right time to critique
   Is not-too-late (v. imp.).

55.

Like shadows from the n-stones at Stonehenge,
   Europe, its nations, is in retrograde,
As if a ghost of honour and revenge
   Is growling in the ears of those dismayed

By fractals of the future, false frontiers
   And far more asking for it than before,
An answer, short and simple, from their fears
   To fences, then an *Anschluss*, then a war.

56.

    Why spy,
    O spi-
        Der, why,
        When I
So confidently click, so scrupulously scroll?

    I'm linked,
    Instinct-
        Ively
        I lie,
I'm pinned, geo-located, like a planet's pole.

    I meet a
    Meta-
        Data
        Doubter,
Why steal what isn't secret? What was it they stole?

    O spooks,
    I speak,
        I like,
        You leak,
I friend, you frame, I share, you shame, I trust, you troll.

    I show,
    Though, so,
        In spies'
        E-eyes,
I am an avatar, an actor in a role.

    So what?
    No whit
        Is nett-
        Ed, not
An *i* of it. A selfie isn't something from the soul.

57.

Arjuna asked, to fight or not to fight,
   In a war against a family of foes,
      What was his calling, what his conscience, what
The cause is of an action that is right.

The cause comes from a brilliant *before*,
   Further before than even time's first throes,
      Like strings that shiver from an arrow's shot,
Although what means a hit or miss is more.

A course of action and its consequences
   Is right or not by *a* plus *b* plus *c*,
      The moment and the motive and the man,
As in the taste of apples, pears or quinces.

And acting from the source of what is right,
   Although it is too bright a light to see,
      The wind of Krishna through his horses' manes,
Arjuna fought as if he didn't fight.

58.

A daughter has to disobey
    And dally in the woods,
Where there are bears, where there are boys,
    To be the woman that she would
    Be, in the wild, wild woods.

A daughter who doesn't disobey,
    Who is a modest maid,
Will be demanding who will buy
    The paper petals she has made,
    When she is mad, is mad.

59.

The quotes!
    We smile, as if we should be spared
The sentence of them for our sins.
    Not quite...
    In thoughts,
    In throats,
These English *sutras* have been shards of sense
    And they have answered and inspired.

60.

I call a corpse a corpse. It seemed to me
    My mother's wasn't my mother anymore
And was a thing, a non-metonymy,
    Mineral almost. Well, no more, no more...

Although a ghost is not allowed to say,
    The *yogis* and Pythagoras have seen
The lights, applause, a set of clouds or clay
    On a new stage and, *Enter*, a new scene.

61.

Out of the early blue, on an Aegean shore,
    His sister, separated, spar and rope
        The only buoying from her brother's berth,
            Sobs on the sand for all her absent ones.

    Orange floaters are heaped along a slope,
        Like lava from the anger of the earth.
Shoes dry, as if outside a prayer room from before.
        A plastic bottle is on the breeze's bounce.

    An old man offers words of help and hope,
        As much hope as a wish to help is worth.
        We were all purple from a passage once,
We were pushed out, in peril, we were washed up ashore.

62.

    The love of listening
To music, has a hush, an upward motion,
        Almost the same
        Ache, the same aim,
      Eyes shut, eyes glistening,
  As unrequited, an untouched emotion.

63.

I trust that neither distance's disguise
    Nor all the difference there is between
Us will make me not matter in your eyes,
    Until what might be is what might have been,

That all the notes we write accumulate
    A fortune, slowly, in a fund of time
That must be mutual to earn a rate
    More than a sentimental sweet *centime*,

        And that these units that I measure with
        Will come to something less than a kiss's width.

64.

The reason why they went to war,
As reasonable as they were,
   Isn't the reason why they fight,
   In rubble, risking snipers' sights
   For micro-motives. Teams are tight.

The reason why the war was fought,
Those feats that wriggled from defeat,
   Isn't the reason why it ends,
   When what x costs and what y spends
   Cancels the losses and amends.

65.

Some of the sentries of the siege
   Are sordid, *Suck our cocks!*
     For a sack of wheat,
     A stack of white
Ampoules of insulin. *Scrounge! Scrounge!*
   A skim-off from their stocks.

Some of the sentries of the siege
   Are strict, no lipstick-dollars,
     Jewels or cash,
     They whip, they cosh
The dolled-up for their sacrilege.
   Death is their only dealer.

66.

The women warriors in green,
   Their barrels still, butts jammed,
Curse through their crosshairs these mad *mujahideen*,
   Die and be damned!

The old town in the dusty light,
   Its skyline dished and domed,
Their pickups rev, as though the engines ululate,
   Die and be damned!

The ruins of a station wall
   That a truck bomb had rammed,
Trails of the fleeing like unravelled wool,
   Die and be damned!

An ochre yard with bones in the soil,
   Where women too old were condemned,
The warriors weep, weep... Their rifles will recoil,
   Die and be damned!

67.

Those rivals of the Renaissance,
Florence and Venice, sent a fleet to fight
The Sultan's, that, despite defeat,
   A setback ever since,
      Seized Cyprus with insulting ease.

The EU uses finances and fences
   That also fail, the files
Of those who flee, who flee, the filth of France's
   Foul camps, the fruit of smiles
      At summits. Compromise/appease.

   And in the ruins of Aleppo,
Turks versus Moors, militia-mercenaries
Versus *jihadi*-janissaries,
   Blowing up dumps and depots,
      Russia rocketing IDPs.

68.

A fifty-something fool,
Who dotes (I won't say *drools*),

And, no, this isn't me
(*C'est moi? Non, mon ami!*),

On someone far too young
For even *yin* and *yang*,

Is yeasty, to deny
A doughy knee and eye.

69.

Imagination, that illuminates,
    Shadows us too, with sub-plots of suspicion,
What hurts dehumanising what it hates,
    With slogans on a placard or petition.

And it conspires, with more-than-metaphors
    Of mutant Tories howling, *Tally-ho!*
The worst of it, the totem of its fears,
    Is what it doesn't say and doesn't know.

70.

   With human evil, I have not
      A faith for fathoming
Where it comes from, if some sub-human will
      Springs up among
Us, seething like a devil in a well.

   With human evil, I have not
      A rational reply
To what is an irrational *don't ask*,
      A lie, a lie,
That hisses like the brain's own basilisk.

   With human evil, I have not
      An empathy enough
For such stone-eyed antipathy,
      O such stern stuff!
With pathos for the puppy on the thigh.

   With human evil, though, I have a plot,
      A history of how
What must destroy must also be destroyed,
      And if not now,
Whenever, vortexed into its own void.

71.

    With human weakness, I will not
        Be over-critical
Of what is only human (even I
        Answer the call
(My flaws won't cost a jeweller an eye)).

    With human weakness, I will not
        Examine what or why,
The long, long list that we explain/excuse,
        Because (and by the way)
It isn't news, it really isn't news.

    With human weakness, I hope what
        The entry-level flaw
That evil uses is is weak enough,
        I.e. good for
Nothing that would do worse with sterner stuff.

72.

With sex, we have to conjugate
   A mood, *have had sex*, past tense, more
     Relaxed, and *having sex*,
  Present continuous (or for
    A good few mins and secs),
And *want sex*, the imperative, that doth invigorate.

What makes us want it is bizarre,
   Either a *burqa* or a basque,
    Although the want *per se*,
  The do-thing, is a bigger ask,
    Bigger than we can say,
Because no sex means no wild odes, no sex means no *beaux arts*.

73.

  A gutter press is looking up
    And shooting down the stars,
      With tuts for tits
      And tits for tuts,
  Pressing for guts, for locking up,
    With shouting down, with stares.

  A minister with mistresses
    Is jailing for a kiss,
      With liars as lawyers
      For lower layers,
  A monster of mistrust, his is
    A jealous fury's curse.

74.

The pear is slumping from its lot,
    The moss is messing up the wall,
She simpered, for a silver pot
    Of sympathy, *He doesn't call.*
The old black beams looked sad and strange,
    The ceiling was awry, the patch
    Of dampness just got damper, *natch,*
Upon the one-bed moated grange.
    Stop whinging, woman, don't be dreary,
        Swim in the moat, I said,
    Go snorkelling, the water's eerie,
        Or row a boat instead.

The sparrows shitting on the roof
    Were whitening the thatch's mound,
A neighbour's hound, its woeful woof,
    Was the silence's own lonely sound,
But Mariana, with a range
    Of feelings further than forlorn,
    Was walking round the weedy lawn
Between the moat's edge and the grange.
    It isn't me that's dreary, dreary,
        It isn't me, she said,
    It's Alfie, it's that bloody bleary
        Poet... O, he's dead.

75.

A heroine,
A-hurryin'
   From task to task to task,

Healin' a king
Of such a t'ing
   Wit' tincture from a tusk,

An' pilgrimin'
To win, amen,
   A man along the way,

Squarin' a ring,
A little wrong,
   At midnight in the hay,

Is waitin' on
The toughest one,
   That ain't no tortoise, ain't no hare,

The knack of it
Or neck of it,
   Makin' him fall in love wit' her,

Tho' if that man
Is minded mean,
   Taskin', even as tough as a tusk,

Is never nuff,
He's rough, he's rough,
   Lovin' as hollow as a husk.

76.

His first war, he was scared,
    As if he was in love
At sixteen, not forever, but the first of many.

His second war, he scored,
    As if he was alive
In action, mercenary, yes, but not for money.

His next war, he was scarred,
    Too caustic to believe
In causes, only in the *machina* of money.

His last war, he was scorched,
    His limbs like blackened loaves,
His DNA unasked-for, one of many, many.

77.

No rights, no rules,
    A ruler who is always right,
The rational response is flattery and fear.

It isn't real,
    Who counsels must conceal, must treat
The truth with what the ruler wants to hear,

And not to rile
    The ruler, he must be adroit,
To halt his hubris now, before its grand nadir.

78.

Who am I? What a question for a king,
   Through all the halls of mirrors of a court,
     That echo endlessly an empty *Yes!*

It isn't dialectical. A king
   Is always right, the orderer of thought,
     The centre and the censor of the news.

Nothing is intimate. An employee
   Is always in the space, has shopped, cooked, cleaned
     And comforted his children in a room.

No fingerprints of his supply his eye
   With sense-coordinates, the *I* aligned.
     His polished palace is an ego-dream.

And when one day a king is not a king,
   The loss is not an answer. *Who am I?*
     He asks, if he is lucky with the loss.

If not, a mob will tell him, mimicking,
   Like mad Gaddafi on his knees. *Not me!*
     He never learned. The mob was merciless.

Or, long hair like a hermit in a hole,
   Is hauled out to be tried for what and why
     And hung for it, no wiser than Saddam.

The vacuum's vastness is a heath of hell,
   A *via negativa* or a way
     Of wondering. *Who am I?* I who am.

79.

To feel
Is more than factual
And, less, to be a fool,
Although, as fun, as fooling,
It isn't ineffectual,
The feeling is fulfilling.

To fool
Is less than factual
And, more, to fail to feel,
Although a common feeling
Isn't contractual,
The fooling is a failing.

80.

And when a storm of light
Is striking through the skull,
A rumble of an *Om*,
The shock is off the scale.

The gut strings are as tight
As a guitar's and twang,
The ground from which a gnome,
Athene-like, once sprang.

81.

The casting for Cordelia is *small*,
    To carry in her corpse. It isn't right.
She was a warrior. Her iron mail
    And spear were gashed and splintered in a rout.

Each region wasn't rich enough alone,
    Marauding to augment its market share,
Or strong enough to stop a rival throne
    Marauding it, a stump of *laissez-faire*.

Is this the way we want it? To divide
    More than a kingdom, end a union,
Vying again, the way these sisters vied,
    With peace *passé*, a poor opinion.

This is the worst, a willingness for war
    That isn't even honest in its aim,
Feuding for flags that feudal forts once wore,
    For game-show glory, for a gore-fest's fame.

82.

These weird ones are a rival rule,
    That men have sworded out,
From their walled O, their *Ur*-authority,
    To rove about,
    To rove about,
With scissors and a stool.

These weird ones are wild worshippers,
    As drunken as devout,
Braids bobbing, in obscene obscurity,
    To reel about,
    To reel about,
While Grey Cat paws and purrs.

83.

The tyrant's wife is taut and tanned,
Her purse as puffy as her pride
    At how this was, not plotted, planned,
A pity that a few protesters died.

And though she seems to condescend,
Honestly, people *should* be nice…
    She knows, if not, how this will end,
Her children will be caught and killed like mice.

She tries. She treats her time with tact-
Ful charm, which charity to choose,
    Which style, which spa, her tummy tucked,
And buys a hundredth pair of happy shoes.

84.

The most efficient means
    Is murder one,
    Is murder one,
The murderous machine's
    Engine is on, for one or more.

Mass mounds in a ravine,
    Then on and on,
    And on and on,
The murderous machine
    Is ratcheted, for more, for more.

Gallows and guillotines,
    No good, no, none,
    No God, no, none,
The murderous machine's
    Pistons are pounding. More, more, more.

85.

A politics of hatred, *red is right*,
Is threaded by a spider of the street
    From lamp posts, letters N, A, I and Z,
    Like heads of idols, upside down and dead.

The oaths of this political occult,
As cloudy as the cauldron of the Celt,
    Are on an ape, a newt, a snake, a sow.
    The scapegoat is the same one, even now.

86.

The sun is red,
   The night is black.

The map is red,
   The book is black.

The flag is red,
   Is red and black.

The shirt is red,
   The boots are black.

The tongue is red,
   The mouth is black.

The knife is red,
   The bullet is black.

The past is red,
   The future is black.

The fire is red,
   The ruins are black.

87.

    To meditate
        When I was young
Was an ascetic yearning, I was lithe
    And lean enough to levitate,
A lark in spirit, blithe-
        Ly called up, if the coil had sprung.

    To meditate
        In middle age
Is more aesthetic, a syrup in the gut,
    More settled too, to gravitate
To what does good, as subt-
        Ly as a *sutra*'s soft massage.

88.

The stains of lubricants on flannel bedding
    Were signs of it, a second adolescence,
        A triumph of tumescence over time.
Think of their big bold boogie at her niece's wedding…

But they were connoisseurs of what they kissed,
    The vintage of it and the evanescence,
        An aftertaste of rosemary and thyme.
The shame was those years wasted, not knowing what they
                                        missed.

89.

O what a man he was, a man
   Who mattered, who was number one.
   The merest mention of his name
Made meetings happen in Milan.

   Night after night, the cocktails, call-girls,
      Flight after flight, the shit-storms, though,
         Had knocked his kidneys out of shape
   And cracked his throat's cloacal growl.

He was a tall man, size twelve shoes,
   A handshake that shook on and on.
   He hushed a hall, filled up its frame,
As if an aide had flipped a fuse.

   The spotlight on him never stopped,
      The shadow of it was a show
         Without an ending, an escape,
   And only lengthened as he stooped.

90.

Bodily beauty isn't why, my friend,
    You will always be beautiful to me,
Though it is in your makeup to amend
      What ages with your style, your health, your sense,
    Like someone from the time of Ptolemy,
      As an exemplar of experience.

Wit isn't why, my so-insightful friend,
    You will always be beautiful to me,
Though the ebullience of it, the end-
      Less brilliance, is beautiful as such
    In you, the liberal economy,
      From word to word, that says so much, so much.

You will always be beautiful to me
    Because of what is always beautiful,
The spill of its Egyptian alchemy,
      The source of wit, the body's aureole,
    Because it is alert, its pulse, its pull.
      What is it that is always beautiful? Your soul.

91.

    A Twitter mob,
        As critical
In mass as in condition,
        Calls for a cull
    Of *them snide snobs,*
A black op of rendition.

    The dispossessed,
        They idly piss
On those whom they abuse,
        Though how they diss,
    As if possessed,
Is worse for women and for Jews.

    The grim old tropes,
        Against the rules
Of grammar, caps on lock,
        When a tweet riles,
    Are trailing ropes
To trap them with. Report and block…

92.

He is polite, professional and *pfff*...
    The point-by-point, the pretty-polly-ticking,
        Through uni, then a spad, then an MP,
    A saucepan with no morsel ever sticking.

He tells me, though, his stats are good, his perf.
    On sub-comms, meeting policies halfway,
        What he is is a pragmatist, small p,
He does things. The applause is not the play.

93.

The power of language, for a populist,
    Is in the lie, the louche hyperbole,
The ugly iambs of a pounding fist
    In poems of unreason, rhyme and rage.

A studied statement on a point of fact
    Is after it, too late, too mannerly...
Which lie? X or its opposite? React!
    The message is the white wig and the rouge.

94.

They called him K, Commander K,
    The cadres, fitting phones to wires
In cellars, oiling old AK-
    47s to fight new wars.

And K said, *Kill the conscripts!* Car
    Bombs blasting outside barracks' gates,
Like bait thrown for the city's curs,
    A shadow showdown with the state.

The state shut shops, smashed martyrs' shrines
    And bulldozed blank lots for its cronies.
The city's businessmen sent signs
    For quiet, not to nuke its crannies.

And K said, *Kill the moderates!*
    A manifesto that was meas-
Urable by the murder rate,
    The roadblocks' rolls of razor mesh.

The centripetal sorting out
    Of who was and was not OK
Kept on, into the last redoubt,
    And K said, *Kill Commander K!*

95.

The photo is *A Sleeping Nude*,
    The painterly and prim-
Rose rays of June's too-early day
    A showcase for her limbs,
    Extended in their own *étude*,
The sheet at low tide, ebbed away.

The sleeping nude did not consent
    To it, she was asleep,
Her breasts' broad areolas staring
    And on the pillow's slope
    Her hair's loose mass (misrepresent-
Ed as) ensouling and ensnaring.

And online it is multiplied,
    Her illegitimate
Image's offspring, never stopp-
    Ing... Maybe it is moot,
    If time, whose eyelids will applaud
Her, won't do worse than Photoshop.

96.

And after all those tragedies
    What could he do
        To get away
    From that dramatic *mi-re-do*
        And that damned question, *why?*
The one-and-only ending, *someone dies.*

He smiled. This is a play, a play,
    A potted plot,
        If not to please,
    At least to try, to try the lot,
        The most unlikely ploys,
Until, haha, it all ends happily.

He wondered. This is new, is now,
    Moment by mo-
        Ment, miming what
    Is not mimetic, *do-re-mi,*
        And doesn't end. The wit
Of it is wise. To know and not to know.

97.

A risk that isn't real
    For them, the knightly chaps,
Is what they run for common-us, wherein,
    As casual collateral
For an old coin, a silver sovereign,
    Is a societal collapse.

My glove, your seconds, sir...
    To satisfy a slight
So slight a handkerchief and *huh* would clean
    The smudge of it, the so-called slur,
The country will disintegrate, decline,
    To *shite*, to utter *shite*.

98.

She picks a stem in pink, in pink,
    And sticks it in the ground to grow,
Like stamens in a breeze, in sync,
    Her dilly-do, sweet dilly-do.

It buzzes like a bee, a bee,
    For pollen in the petals' O,
Speeding up uncontrollably,
    Her dilly-do, sing, dilly-do.

99.

Nobody chooses to be changed,
    To a strange human stone,
        After the soul is wronged,
To be so used to it, to be estranged,
        The pain of it to be prolonged.

Nobody chooses not to change
    From that, a standing stone,
        For sixteen or more years,
More chiselled anyway, more struck, more strange,
        With what perversely perseveres.

Nobody chooses. Even so,
    To step out of that stone,
        After so long, so long,
To something that is moving, softly, slow-
    Ly, seems a blessing, to atone
        For what was wrong, still wrong,
And with a subtle sweetness to bestow
        This bliss on us, when we belong.

100.

This island isn't England, it is hot
    And oozy, ooh,
Mangoes, papayas, and from space a spot
    Of chlorophyll amidst a royal blue.

This England isn't an island, it is not,
    The wet Welsh hills,
The Highlands of the eagle and the Scot
    Abut. Ah, but a *blot* of this is Bill's...

This island isn't an island, it is dot-
    Dot-dot, a pix-
Elated paradise the world forgot
    Or not (the clicks of plots, of politics).

101.

This monster is of man, but isn't man,
    Of mind, but not of meaning, not of matter,
As murky and misshapen as a moan
    Is, a miasma. *Mutter, mutter, mutter...*

*

This monster is an eel, an oily tongue,
Of what is sunless, slippery and wrong.
    Because it must be right, be black-and-white,
    It slices coldly, bite by bite by bite.

*

This monster is an *animus* of speech,
Shouting abuse, a bully-beast who boos
At bubble-bursters, bringers of bad news.
    Its politics is personal, a *putsch*.

102.

O Ariel,
>Through whom the air
Coheres, in iambs, like a line
>>Of light a laser writes, a reel
>>>Of footage on which are
Such shapes, such shadows, as will shine,

>A sunny isle,
>>So many seas
Away, is an immediate
>>>Image of sound, a .wav file,
>>>>With coral in its keys,
That scallop speakers mediate,

>An *Om*-like call,
>>As if to ask
For ether, is a catch of the
>>>Uncanny, in a magical
>>>>Old metaphor, a masque,
In which the actors' auras seem to breathe,

>And the effect
>>On those who hear
Is a transformative soul-change,
>>>A shanty's *shanti*, an inflect-
>>>>Ed calling to cohere,
That is transcendent, *rich and strange*.

103.

A work of art, then, if it works,
    Is what it works on us,
As artist and as audience, that thing
    That thrills us more than, ahem, twerks
        Or treatises, because
It is the *atman* that is authoring.

    Against that, human nature isn't an
        Artistic animal
And answers this aesthetic transformation
    With apathy, a temper tan-
        Trum and with something small
And anti-spacey (for your information).

    A harmony of human na-
        Ture and the work of art
Is an attainment, an unending task,
    That has its habits, as in a
        Symbolic staff, to start
With, a white book, a willingness to ask.

Notes

Playful Poems is a sequence of short poems that was written between March 2015 and August 2016, prompted by reading most of Shakespeare's plays in their likely chronological order.

1-3.	*The Taming Of The Shrew*
4-8.	*Richard III*
9-10.	*The Comedy Of Errors*
11-12.	*Love's Labour's Lost*
13-16.	*Richard II*
17-20.	*Romeo And Juliet*
21-25.	*A Midsummer Night's Dream*
26-29.	*The Merchant Of Venice*
30-33.	*Henry IV Part One*
34-36.	*Henry IV Part Two*
37-38.	*The Merry Wives Of Windsor*
39-40.	*Much Ado About Nothing*
41-45.	*Henry V*
46-50.	*Julius Caesar*
51-53.	*As You Like It*
54-60.	*Hamlet*
61-63.	*Twelfth Night*
64-66.	*Troilus And Cressida*
67-71.	*Othello*
72-74.	*Measure For Measure*
75-76.	*All's Well That Ends Well*
77-81.	*King Lear*
82-86.	*Macbeth*
87-90.	*Antony And Cleopatra*
91-94.	*Coriolanus*
95-96.	*Cymbeline*
97-99.	*The Winter's Tale*
100-103.	*The Tempest*

7. *cast the die*
Richard III, Act 5, Scene 3, Lines 363-364:
"Slave, I have set my life upon a cast,
And I will stand the hazard of the die."

21. Wild times! I know a ditch in Walthamstow
A Midsummer Night's Dream, Act 2, Scene 1, Line 244:
"I know a bank where the wild thyme blows,"

52. *of formal cut*
As You Like It, Act 2, Scene 7, Lines 155-157:
"And then the justice,
In fair round belly with good capon lined,
With eyes severe and beard of formal cut,"

74. is a pastiche of Tennyson's *Measure For Measure* prequel poem *Mariana*.

100. *blot*
Richard II, Act 2, Scene 1, Lines 40-64:
"this sceptred isle...
This blessed plot, this earth, this realm, this England...
With inky blots"

102. *rich and strange*
The Tempest, Act 1, Scene 2, Lines 460-464:
"Of his bones are coral made:
Those are pearls that were his eyes:
Nothing of him that doth fade,
But doth suffer a sea-change
Into something rich and strange."

PLAYFUL POEMS

Andrew Staniland's *Playful Poems* is a sequence of over a hundred short poems written between March 2015 and August 2016 and prompted by reading most of Shakespeare's plays in their likely chronological order. There are poems about the wars in Ukraine and Syria, refugees, dictators, nationalism and Brexit, as well as *The lovely wood of piebald light/That any English poem is.*

Rhapsodies (2014)

Andrew Staniland's *Rhapsodies (2014)* takes its title from the verse form of the two long poems at its centre, *Rhapsody* and *Corona Lumina*, written in long rhyming couplets. The same verse form is used for a poem about the Ukrainian musicians *Dakh Daughters* and Valentin Silvestrov. There are translations from Russian and Ukrainian, a tribute to Seamus Heaney and a sequence of short poems about an album by the French singer-songwriter Amélie-les-crayons.

The Perennial Poetry (2010)

Andrew Staniland's *The Perennial Poetry (2010)* is a collection of contemporary English Romantic poetry written in classical metre. There are poems about spiritual experience, creativity, love and poetry itself. The subjects include contemporary films and paintings, Chartres cathedral and the war in Afghanistan, a trip to Tallinn and writing a themed poem for a poetry competition. There are odes and sonnets, including translations of French, Spanish, Italian and German sonnets.

Two Story Poems (2009)

Andrew Staniland's *Two Story Poems (2009)* are original stories in classical verse. *A Human Disguise* is a spiritual comedy set in ancient India. A minor god takes on human form to hide from a demon who is chasing him. *Compassion* is a ghost story set in medieval Japan. A *samurai* gains a supernatural power that is too terrible for him to use.

HYMNS, FILMS AND SONNETINAS (2007)

Andrew Staniland's *Hymns, Films And Sonnetinas (2007)* are written in classical metre, in the romantic tradition of English poetry. They include *Five Hymns* (dedicated to five gods and goddesses representing different elements of contemporary culture and spirituality), *Twelve Films By Eric Rohmer*, *An Older Actress* (a narrative poem in alexandrine couplets about a French actress and her film career), *William Blake And The Eighteenth Century New Age* and *Sonnetinas* (a miscellaneous sequence of sonnet-like miniatures).

NEW POEMS (2006)

The poems in Andrew Staniland's *New Poems (2006)* are poems about contemporary spiritual experience, written in classical metre, in the romantic tradition of English poetry. They include a series of odes and a sequence of short poems which give the collection its title.

THE BEAUTY OF PSYCHE (2005)

Andrew Staniland's prose-poem novel *The Beauty Of Psyche (2005)* is a retelling of the Greek myth of Cupid and Psyche as a novel about imagination. The characters are played by actors, against a backdrop of paintings, models and sets. The story at times becomes a series of paintings and sculptures in an exhibition. And the references to people, films, theatre and other myths may or may not be imaginary too.

The Weight Of Light (2004)

Andrew Staniland's prose-poem novel *The Weight Of Light (2004)* is a lyrical description of the inner life and spiritual practice of Delphine, a Frenchwoman living in London. It is set entirely in her apartment, like a camera recording the poetry of her daily life, her meditations and spiritual experiences. It is a "new spirituality" novel that is both literary and an honest description of a contemporary spiritual life.

Three Cine-Poems (1997)

The three cine-poems collected here use classical blank verse and contemporary cinematic narrative techniques to tell their stories.

White Russian (1995) is a lyrical description of a young Russian woman's life in London.

A Child Of God (1996) is a comic study of a New Age guru and his small band of devotees.

A European Master (1997) is a debate about contemporary aesthetic values between a French actress and an East European film director.

POEMS (1982-2004)

This is a collection of Andrew Staniland's poems from 1982 to 2004. Some are written in free verse, some in metric verse. They are in the romantic tradition of English poetry and explore contemporary spiritual and psychotherapeutic experience.

Four Plays (1994)

The Temple Of The Goddess (1992) is a verse tragedy set in pre-classical Greece. A matriarchal bronze age state is invaded by a patriarchal iron age army.

The Playwright (1993) is a drama about resurgent nationalism in post-communist Eastern Europe.

Mornings In The Life Of A Theatre Critic (1993) is a London theatre comedy.

The Valley Of Stones (1994) is a tragedy of survival and defiance in a refugee camp.